# A Head Full of Stories

First published 2005
Evans Brothers Limited
2A Portman Mansions
Chiltern Street
London W1U 6NR

Text copyright © Evans Brothers Limited 2005
© in the illustrations Tim Archbold 2005

British Library Cataloguing in Publication Data
Swallow, Su
        A head full of stories. - (Twisters)
        1. Children's stories - Pictorial works
        I. Title
        823.9'14 [J]

ISBN-10: 0237530708
13-digit ISBN (from 1 January 2007) 9780237530709

Printed in China by WKT Company Limited

Series Editor: Nick Turpin
Design: Robert Walster
Production: Jenny Mulvanny
Series Consultant: Gill Matthews

# A Head Full of Stories

## Su Swallow
## and Tim Archbold

Evans

"Jack!"

"Story time!"

"No!" shouted Jack.
"My head is full up with stories."

"You tell
me a story,
then."

So Jack told Mum about
Cinderella.

He told Dad a story too.

# And Grandma…

and Grandad…

# and his brother...

and the cat...

and Teddy.

"My head's empty now!"

# "Tell me a story please!"

Why not try reading another Twisters book?

**Not-so-silly Sausage** by Stella Gurney and Liz Million
ISBN 0 237 52875 4

**Nick's Birthday** by Jane Oliver and Silvia Raga
ISBN 0 237 52896 7

**Out Went Sam** by Nick Turpin and Barbara Nascimbeni
ISBN 0 237 52894 0

**Yummy Scrummy** by Paul Harrison and Belinda Worsley
ISBN 0 237 52876 2

**Squelch!** by Kay Woodward and Stefania Colnaghi
ISBN 0 237 52895 9

**Sally Sails the Seas** by Stella Gurney and Belinda Worsley
ISBN 0 237 52893 2

**Billy on the Ball** by Paul Harrison and Silvia Raga
ISBN 0 237 52926 2

**Countdown** by Kay Woodward and Ofra Amit
ISBN 0 237 52927 0

**One Wet Welly** by Gill Matthews and Belinda Worsley
ISBN 0 237 52928 9

**Sand Dragon** by Su Swallow and Silvia Raga
ISBN 0 237 52929 7

**Cave-baby and the Mammoth** by Vivian French and Lisa Williams
ISBN 0 237 52931 9

**Albert Liked Ladders** by Su Swallow and Barbara Nascimbeni
ISBN 0 237 52930 0

**Molly is New** by Nick Turpin and Silvia Raga
ISBN 0 237 53067 8

**Head Full of Stories** by Su Swallow and Tim Archbold
ISBN 0 237 53069 4

**Elephant Rides Again** by Paul Harrison and Liz Million
ISBN 0 237 53073 2

**Bird Watch** by Su Swallow and Simona Dimitri
ISBN 0 237 53071 6

**Pip Likes Snow** by Lynne Rickards and Belinda Worsley
ISBN 0 237 53075 9

**How to Build a House** by Nick Turpin and Barbara Nascimbeni
ISBN 0 237 53065 1